Making "Work" Work for You:

Tips, Hacks, and Strategies for Finding Career Bliss

By Kris McPeak

*Dedicated to all the Housing Professionals
(and Recovering Housing Professionals)
who have inspired me to be my best self.*

Table of Contents
Introduction – Wisdom from 9 Jobs in 7 States
Chapter One – Talkin' About My Generation
Chapter Two – How Did I Get Here?
Chapter Three - Daily Hacks, Blissful Habits, and DIY Development
Chapter Four - Relationships
Chapter Five - How Many Ways Can You Be Away and Still Be Okay?
Chapter Six – Should I Stay or Should I Go?
Conclusion

Introduction:
Wisdom from 9 Jobs in 7 States

"I'm taking what they're giving 'cause I'm working for a living."
--Huey Lewis and the News
"I don't want to work; I want to bang on the drum all day."
--Todd Rundgren
"Working 9 to 5, what a way to make a living."
--Dolly Parton
"Give me a job, give me security, give me a chance to survive."
--Styx

I guess that you bought this book because one of these sets of song lyrics resonates with you slightly. Maybe you are new to the workforce, or maybe you have been in it one way or another for decades. Maybe you are a blue collar worker doing shift work and living paycheck to paycheck. Perhaps you are a corporate genius trying to build a family. Or perchance you are a cubicle jockey who didn't get the memo about the TPS Reports. But you could be like me, having worked at colleges and universities your entire adult life. I built my career around higher education, and I haven't looked back.

Did I graduate high school with a plan to work at a college for the rest of my life? Of course not. I went to college thinking that I was going to become a teacher; after graduation, I thought I wanted to become a guidance counselor. By the time I graduated with my Master's Degree in 1994, I had decided to become a Student Affairs Professional.

What is that, you ask? According to NASPA (Student Affairs Administrators in Higher Education), the field of student affairs consists of professional staff members whose job "is to foster and promote interactions [among students]. Encouraging an understanding and respect for diversity, a belief the worth of individuals, and supporting our students in their needs are just some of the core concepts of the profession.

Why did I choose it? Many of my contemporaries would say, "I didn't choose this field, it chose me." My sophomore year of college, I became a Resident Advisor in my residence hall (or, dorm, if we must). I loved how that job made me feel. I loved planning events for my students, making posters and door decorations, and helping them when they were in need. Monthly staff developments taught me some new skill sets and let me socialize with Resident Advisors in other halls. However, what I really loved was the free room and board...I'm not gonna lie about that. But as I started to tell my own students later in life, "You'll *take* this job for the free room and board; but you'll *keep* this job because it will change your life."

So, since 1994, I've worked at 9 colleges in 7 states. I've worked at small private colleges, large state schools, community colleges, urban and suburban institutions...you name it, I've probably worked there. And in those 20+ years, I've learned a great deal about professionalism, what matters most in your life's work, how to find employment and keep it, and work/life balance. Not all at once...and not in an instant. But if I could go back and do it all again, I would definitely have done things differently. And that is why I decided to write this book.

"Making Work *Work* for You" does not just talk about achieving work/life balance. I am going to challenge your choices regarding your current position. I will get you to think about your support networks and how to structure your work day more comfortably. Hopefully, none of you will need Chapters 4 and 5, but they are there for you should you reach that point in your professional life. Although I think from time to time, we all question our vocation, so these chapters might just solidify why you want to stay where you are now. I hope so. That would make me so happy for you.

I am thoroughly enjoying my career as an educator, even during the years where I struggled with the Blurred Lines, Unrealistic Expectations, and Impractical Multitasking. A study by Gail Kinman and Siobhan Wray in July of 2013 stated that three-quarters of educators work more than 40 hours a week with about one-third working more than 50 hours a week. There are plenty of other professions that can claim the same, so I know I'm not alone in believing we work too damn much or we can't get our work done during the day, making the extra hours required. Enough already. This is no way to live. And that is why I was drawn to start writing this book.

During the time I finished this book, I was going through a period of reflection and journaling, and watching a good number of webinars on self-publishing and reading a ton on law of attraction stuff. So at the very last minute, I opted to include reflection questions for each of the chapters. I hope you will take the time to do the reflection and journaling; I think it will really help you get on the right path to finding Your Career Bliss.

Finally, I hope that all who are drawn to this book will have a collective understanding that my lessons are not just for New Professionals in the field of student affairs. I will often speak from that point of view because that is my experience. As far as I'm concerned, these lessons, tips, and stories apply to everyone in the workforce. And I'm just optimistic enough to think that lawyers, doctors, creatives, web designers, construction workers, truck drivers, and entrepreneurs can benefit from this book as well.
So settle in, and let's see if I can help you find that career bliss…

Chapter One
Talkin' About My Generation

With which Generation do you identify? Sure, you may already have been tagged as one thing or another; as an adult, I've developed the mindset that I can own any trait or personality type that I want. This is most definitely why I did not want to claim Generation X as my own when it was first identified and branded, if you will. When that label first hit the mainstream, I was just finishing grad school and heading into my first full time job. And everyone was calling the Gen X'ers a bunch of cynical, lazy, unmotivated slackers. Or, as Juliana Hatfield sang:

You might think we all need that stuff, but I don't think about it much...
I was born of people's needs, and what they don't want to believe
But I am a liar, and that's the truth, go home and think it through
That's the harm in mystery, all you know is what you see
I got no idols...

Well, I did have idols. Quite a few, in fact, and they weren't only my parents. I didn't feel cynical or self-involved as many sociologists were suggesting. I believed I was very loyal and had a deep sense of mission. I didn't think I was working in a dead-end job. I saw myself as highly motivated. And I wasn't crazy about Nirvana or Pearl Jam. So this Gen X label upset me. Those were my sister's people, not mine.

Turns out, I was wrong. Gen X'ers were born between 1965 and 1984, so I'm right at the beginning of this generation having been born in 1968 (The Atlantic, March 25, 2014). A Generational Differences chart as published by the West Midland Family Center indicates that my generation's influencers were Watergate, the Energy Crisis, coming from blended and dual income families, and being latchkey kids. We grew up having to take care of ourselves, and we came of age when the USA was losing its status as the most powerful and prosperous nation in the world. We were unimpressed with authority but were self-disciplined. We yearn for new skill sets and are the least idealistic of the living generations.

And according to this chart, our core values list balance first. Our attributes include flexibility and independence. Our work ethic and values state, "Care less about advancement than about work/life balance." We work hard AND play hard. And we know that sometimes you need to make Work into Play.

In the article "Common Characteristics of Generation X Professionals" (The Balance), we are individualistic, technologically adept, flexible, value work/life balance, and we incorporate humor and games into the workplace. According to Dan Schawbel's blog post, "44 of the Most Interesting Facts about Generation X," we rank workplace flexibility as the most important perk of our jobs, we eventually want to become entrepreneurs, and we are unique in our work ethic.

Can ya feel me on this?

Generation X cares the most about working smarter, not harder, having the freedom to manage our time and work, wanting an empowered workforce that can manage our hard work with our downtime. We're independent, pragmatic, and self-reliant. We value the individual, and we want to nurture relationships.

If you identify with Generation X, listen up. Because you have a responsibility.

But What About Millennials? Do They Have a Responsibility?

Sheltered. Helicopter Parents. 9/11 was a major influencer.

"Ambitious but not entirely focused. Look to the workplace for direction and to help them achieve their goals."

"Expect to influence the terms and conditions of the job."

"Have a work ethic that no longer mandates 10 hour days."

Now that the Baby Boomers are retiring, Generation X is rising to Senior Management level; and Millennials are just getting into management and middle management. These two generations have a responsibility to steer the ship and navigate away from the workaholic culture that retiring executives have role modeled for the past twenty years. Hard work does not have to equate to being a workaholic. The internal pressure to work harder all the time is hurting us and if I know one thing right now, in 2017…we need to take it easy and take care of ourselves.

Reflection Questions
1. What have you been taught about your generation and its profile? Do you agree or disagree with the traits?
2. What did your parents/guardians model for you about employment, jobs, and work? Do your values align with theirs? Why or why not?

Chapter 2
How Did I Get Here?
AKA, "I got kids to feed, Jack."

"And you may find yourself
Living in a shotgun shack
And you may find yourself
In another part of the world
And you may find yourself
Behind the wheel of a large automobile
And you may find yourself in a beautiful house
With a beautiful wife
And you may ask yourself, well
How did I get here?"
--Talking Heads

Let's first get a sense of where you are now and if you are in a good situation. Hopefully, many of you can actually stop reading this book when this chapter is complete. That would tell me that you've got a good thing going on at your current gig.

However, my guess is that you bought this book because you feel out of balance, you are burned out, or you are considering a career transformation but don't know how to start. So let's work through what you've got going on now and see where things need to change.

Why did you choose your current job?
In my 20+ years of working at colleges and universities, no one instinctively "chooses" student affairs. We fall into it. Because we go to college and we get involved in some way. We become a Resident Advisor, or we join a fraternity or sorority, or we run for Student Government....and naturally there's an advisor or professor who mentors us and finally says, "Have you thought about getting into student affairs?" It's not a career you know about from your grade school years and talk about during Show and Tell. Granted, there ARE children being raised in Residence Halls who may very well go to school and talk about being awakened in the middle of the night by something loud and annoying...and yet they see the gratitude and pride in their parents' faces so they think about what it would be like for them in this career. Maybe they DO go to school and say, "When I grow up, I want to be a Hall Director."

In fact, there are quite a few jobs out there that we have no idea exists when we are in high school, college, graduate school, and beyond. How many of you were aware of such nifty positions as a headhunter, social media coordinator, recreational manager, sustainability coordinator, compliance officer, or logistician? My little "School Years" scrapbook did not list these jobs in the "What do you want to be when you grow up?" section. What was usually listed was doctor, nurse, fireman, policeman, lawyer, teacher, and farmer.

In the film "Election" (1999, Alexander Payne), Jim McAllister (Matthew Broderick), our narrator, tells the audience about his friend Dave Novotny (Mark Harelik). Dave was someone who became a high school teacher because he never really wanted to leave high school in the first place. While that ended badly for Dave in the movie, it's a very similar situation as to why some of us fell into the world of Student Affairs: we truly LOVED every single experience about college and just weren't ready to leave. That's not the best reason, but inevitably we find something about the gig that we really connect with, and then when that mentor tells us that this is a real career...well...there you have it. "You mean, I can get paid to make posters and door decorations and plan parties and run elections?" Yes, you can.

Taking time to reflect on why you have chosen your current job can definitely aid in finding work and life balance. Do you think you chose your career because it's what you really wanted? Maybe a mentor or supervisor told you, "you'd be really good at this, you should go to graduate school." Did you become a Resident Advisor and then a Hall Director and whatever else came next for you, and you aren't sure that you're qualified to do anything else? Have you been doing whatever you are doing for so long that you can no longer fathom getting out or making a career change? Or – dare I ask - are you in a career that someone else chose for you?

There are many people out in the world who don't have job satisfaction or engagement because they really don't know why they are in that field in the first place. I love and respect actor Morgan Freeman and recall his acceptance speech when he received the Cecil B. DeMille Lifetime Achievement Award from the Hollywood Foreign Press in 2012. "It's been said, if you do what you love, you'll never work a day in your life." I'm sure he wasn't the first person to say that; if you do a Google search, you can find all sorts of memes and inspirational images that you can post on your Instagram. And I think he's exactly right.

How many of us wake up and really forward going to our job? Do you jump into your car with giddy anticipation of what lies ahead? Or do you drag your ass to the car and let out a sigh of complete defeat because you can't possibly fathom having to go to "that place" one more day?

Craig Nathanson (trans4mind.com) defines the difference between job and vocation and the difference is pretty clear. A job has a defined description of duties, mostly written by others. It has pre-defined working hours and a set wage. Jobs have non-value added activities like email and meetings. In jobs, you compete rather than collaborate, and it doesn't always align with your personal values. If you wanna get a little religious with this, consider the biblical figure Job – same spelling, different pronunciation. The United States Conference of Catholic Bishops describes the Book of Job as "an exquisite dramatic treatment of the problem of the suffering of the innocence." Suffering. Ouch.

A vocation, however, means you are doing work that fits you. You will never "retire" from a vocation. You don't have to prepare for work because it comes naturally. You create your own development path and don't need approval from others. You get paid for using your natural gifts, and you look forward to every meeting and every email because it validates your great work. I think you get the point. You can focus on your craft and set the artist free.

Just like "Cosmic Shame" by Tenacious D. Look it up on YouTube. This song is about setting the artist free. Supposedly. And while Jack Black and Kyle Gass may have a raunchier and narcissistic view on how this all goes down, the underlying logic is solid.

"Focus on your craft, one time, before it's all over, you've died, you've squandered it, you fuckin' robots!"

Easier said than done, right. *"I got kids to feed, Jack."* I need to pay rent and my bills and eat and have a life. You are absolutely right. You totally do. But you won't find equilibrium between work and life if you hate your job so much that you come home and do nothing but reflect on the awful, tiring, frustrating days while you make your family and friends miserable. You do not need to suffer to live your life.

If someone asked you the question, "do you love your vocation so much that you'd do it for free," how would you answer?
Consider some of these questions, and do some reflecting, or write in a journal:
    a. Why did I go to college in the first place?
    b. Am I even using my degree as it was intended?
    c. What do I love about my current gig?
    d. What do I wish I could let go in the current gig?
    e.

There was really not an option for me about going to college. I was going. Well, actually, I recall telling my father that I would be attending So-and-so University with the majority of my friends, and his response being something along the lines of, "No, you will attend your state university." I didn't know enough about colleges at that time to argue the point. Plus, my high school sweetheart was going there. I had a high school English teacher that I really admired, so heading to the University of Arkansas I declared English as my major. That was in the fall semester. In the spring semester of my freshman year, I changed my major to Secondary Education because my boyfriend and I had a plan. I should teach while he attends medical school and then start having babies. But that's the topic of another book.

My point is, that when you are 18 years old, you don't really have a sense of what you want to do or who you want to be. I've worked in higher education long enough to see that in action every single year. I recall the first year chemistry classes with 300 students registered; but after the first exam, that number dropped to about 175 or so. When I was in college in the late 80's/early 90's, the average college student changed their major 7 times. SEVEN. Currently, the University of Laverne suggests that the average college student will change their major at least three times before they graduate. Borderzine.com says that college students will continue to change their major until they find something they love. The Shorthorn (University of Texas at Arlington) cites ten reasons students change their major, including lack of encouragement to explore, positive experiences, and money vs. passion. Did Mom and Dad hammer you in high school to be a lawyer, but the minute you took that film class to fulfill an art requirement, you suddenly found your educational appetite? Did you finally ditch the accounting major once you joined the Critical Theory Club and decided that you wanted to teach? College is absolutely, positively a place where you get your education and identify your vocation, but it's also where you grow up. My father DID tell me that he didn't care if I graduated or not. He was sending me to college to become "a fully functional adult member of society," where I would learn how to pay my bills, stand up for myself, and contribute to the economy. The rest was all up to me, and whatever made me happy (my dad was so awesome in this way, he should have been a coach or teacher or something).

Let's get back to that "When You Are 18 Years Old" thing. Maybe your roommate was that student who found all the parties on the first day of Freshman Orientation. And almost never went to class. And had a stash of pot under the mattress. And got put on academic probation. And used the spring tuition money to pay for a spring break trip. Maybe...you were that student. You can't get a refund on your tuition paid, and you have to move back home. Or just get a job and an apartment. That is a wasted semester (or year, or two years, depending on the student's situation). If your parents fronted your college money, then they are both pissed off and disappointed. But if you had grants, loans, or scholarships, then those funds were indeed squandered, never to be seen again. Bummer.

This one of the main reasons why I really believe in what community colleges have to offer. Tuition is much less expensive than four-year schools, and many of them have Open Enrollment, which means you can register at any time. Community Colleges, in my experience, are also not overly selective, so everyone gets accepted. You can usually find a good balance of academic programs and career/technical programs. And in many cases, the career/technical education programs outnumber the academic ones. My Career Bliss is currently at a community college where I run a scholarship program for a foundation, among other things. My true Gen-X self is thrilled because I get to learn new skill sets all the time. I meet all sorts of students in my work, and they come from every possible walk of life. First generation college students, International Students, students who are poor and students who are rich. Some of the most amazing and dedicated students I have met are the Returning Students. This group of students is usually removed five years or more from high school, and they come to community college for a number of reasons:

    a. Never finished college the first time and are coming back to get a degree
    b. Finished college, hated their first job (second job, third job, etc.), and are coming back to reinvent themselves
    c. Started college, got married and had children, and want to explore life-long learning to set an example for the kids.

I love returning students. They have lived life, and most of them have a very specific understanding of what they want out of their current academic or vocational program. Many still have plans to get that four-year degree, but it's not unheard of that they pursue career program certificates that allow them to get right back into the workforce, usually doing something they have absolutely learned to love and want to do for the rest of their lives. Sweet.
I took the long way around in starting to suggest why we aren't usually ready to decide what to do with our lives at the age of 18. And once again, if you picked up this book then you probably are looking to find some bliss in your current gig, or you are figuring that it's time to reflect on why you're in that position. Ask yourself these questions:

How did I get here?
How long have I been here?
Why am I afraid to leave?
Do I see a happy future in this position?

Talk to someone you trust about your thoughts and feelings. And if the answers to those questions suggest you need to move on, it's time to consider this. We'll cover the next steps in another chapter.

Defining and Understanding the Culture of Your Employer
For those of you in higher education, this is what we call Institutional Culture. Or Organizational Culture. Or Corporate Culture. What we are talking about here is the nature of the way things work at your place of business. These are the customs, rituals, and values that a new person must accept during his tenure there. It is often implied rather than defined and can develop progressively over time from the collective traits of the employees hired.

It may take months, even years to pin this down anywhere. And for people in higher education who may change jobs every two years or so for promotional purposes, you may never really be able to put your finger on it. But it's worth your time to understand as much as you can about this before you accept the job.

Yes, you are going to have to do copious research when applying for positions. Start with the job description and see if a mission or vision statement is listed. What does the organization value outwardly? If you can't find this in a job description, you can surely find it on the organization or institutions webpage.

Frankly, if you aren't trolling that webpage for everything you can, you aren't really preparing. Again, that job description should also tell you the various departments, divisions, or offices where your specific position is housed.

For example…
University of Career Bliss – Organization/Institution
Vice-President of Work/Life Balance – Executive Management
Director of Vocational Happiness – Senior Management
Assistant Director for Fulfilled Employees – Middle Management
Coordinator of Professional Contentment – Entry Level
Etc.

The position you are pursuing could be any of these samples or something else in between. Understanding the organizational structure gives you a baseline for where all the other stuff fills in.
Let's say you applied for the Assistant Director for Fulfilled Employees position. You have the job description, and now you know where the position is housed. So your next step is to the division page of Work/Life Balance. They probably have their own vision or mission statement, or at least some kind of definition of what function they perform for the organization. Finally, there may also be a welcome or greeting from the Senior Manager in that area, and that is worth reading as well.

So you've done your basic research on the employer, and you've read that job description over and over. Now you want to get ready for your interview day. You are actually interviewing the employer as much as they are interviewing you. You aren't doing yourself any favors if you go to an interview unprepared – and what I really mean is knowing what you need to ask in order to determine if this gig is a good fit for you.

My professional interview experience is very different from that of my corporate, retail, and business friends. I am accustomed to spending an entire day, sometimes two days, interviewing with various different groups and constituencies who are stakeholders in helping select the candidate who will be offered the job. And I've been spoiled in that almost every interview I've attended has provided me with an interview schedule and a list of staff or students with whom I'd be meeting. So, yes, this is a gift and a great way to fully prepare for your interview experience.

If you have this chance, you can prepare your interview questions unique for each group. Depending on the level of the position, you'd probably be meeting Senior Management, Middle Management and Entry Level, supervisees, administrative staff, or students. You can contact me directly if you would like various sample questions to use in your preparation.

<u>What values are most deeply held by Senior Management?</u>
When interviewing at a college or university, you should get some face time with The Big Boss - a Director, VP, Dean, etc. It could be a lunch, and it could be a 15-minute sit-down. For a corporate or retail position, you may or may not have face time with a senior manager; but unless you are interviewing with a recruiter, there should still be someone that's part of your interview experience who leads the charge for that department or division. Hopefully, you do have time to ask at least one question. Some ideas might be:

i. What do you value most in your employees?
ii. What do you expect from your team?
iii. How can I best contribute to this department?

These are some of my favorites; they are easy to remember, and for a short, basic question you can get a good amount of insight. Take good note of how they respond. Answers that include, "hard work," "loyalty," or "persistence/determination" could also translate into "Long Hours," or "Sell Me Your Soul." But if the answers are more like, "creativity," "honesty," and "unique thinking," then maybe this is a culture of flexibility and expression.

Is There Room for Advancement?
Many higher education websites will list the full staff on their homepage, so you can study the team composition and see where you lie within the department structure. In some cases, websites may feature biographies, so you can get a sense of where people went to school, how long they've been in their current position, and how long they've been at the institution. This is all good information to just have in the back of your mind. During an interview, you may have the chance to ask a future peer or teammate, "is it easy to move up in this department?" and get a sense of whether the culture favors longevity, or if you need to move on to move up. In the retail or corporate world, you may want to wait and ask this question during your final interview or once an offer is made and you are negotiating salary, etc.

Holidays, Closures, Breaks, Vacation
Because as noted in the chapter on vacation, we Americans don't take enough because the general culture does not support it. You still need to know, because taking vacation time contributes greatly to your work/life balance. First of all, if you are interviewing for a position academia, check the college/university search engine and look for "college closings" or "academic calendar." You should be able to get a sense of when the college is open and when it's closed. Another search of the Human Resources page may even feature a memorandum of holidays for the academic/fiscal year.

If you are not interviewing for a position in higher education, then this may be tougher information to locate prior to your interview, but even a corporation's website should have some human resources information available.

It may seem obvious that federal holidays are recognized everywhere. Do not make this assumption. My college holidays have been different at every single institution I've worked. One place will recognize President's Day, but you'll work Veteran's Day. One place will be open for Labor Day but will close for Spring Break. There are so many possible combinations. I reached a point in my career where I told myself I could never work at a college/university that did NOT have a winter break closure. In the corporate world or private sector, this almost never happens.

What you probably won't find on an employer's website is when you can or cannot take vacation. If you are pursuing a position at a college or university, you probably will not ever be able to take vacation during the month where classes begin - or the month during commencement activities. Unless you have a life-event like a wedding or family reunion and you schedule it with your supervisor way in advance. I have a friend who works for a state department of education, and her busy months are July and September/October. So it definitely varies, and you'll probably want to know what your employer's preference is to determine if the place is a good fit for you. This information can probably be handled during an interview with your future peers/colleagues/teammates, or with your supervisor. I once had to cancel my anniversary plans due to a new student banquet taking place on the same weekend. I was new at this position and didn't have a lot of credibility with my team or supervisor yet.

<u>Political Hot Buttons – You Just Don't Ask About That Because…</u>
I'm still not sure if I even want to keep this section in the book. Because determining political issues at your place of employment may not be something you can ask about during an interview, but it could very well be something that creeps up over time, and if you don't know how to navigate through these hot buttons, you could wind up in a pickle. I recall starting a new position at an institution where a high-ranking administrator of the college had made quite a few enemies within the faculty, and it was taking a toll on the campus. Sides were being taken, and there were morale problems everywhere. If you find yourself in a very trusting position with your supervisor, or you've made a Vital Work Friend with whom you can confide, you may be able to get a sense of why some of these hot buttons exist and why they are problematic. Or you may just want to stay out of the way.

<u>Reflection Questions:</u>
    a. Answer the questions posed to you starting on Page 11 and again on Page 14.
    b. Consider your current employer and see if you can write down what you think the institutional culture represents.

Chapter Three
Daily Hacks, Blissful Habits, and DIY Development

Okay, so you know that you're in a job that fulfills you – but it's not necessarily your vocation yet, and you don't really need to Vote with Your Feet yet. If you still struggle to get through the work day, you're not completely engaged, and/or you're feeling overworked or underappreciated, I promise, there is hope. There are small fixes you can engage in that can mitigate some of the funk and sustain you until you're ready for the next thing.

Being intentional on how you schedule your time.
You may have one of those jobs in which one could easily be in meetings for a full day, leaving very little time to actually get your work done. Staff meetings, senior management meetings, committee meetings, supervisory meetings (also called One-on-One's), disciplinary meetings...this list goes on and on. During my years as a Manager and Senior Manager, I was in meetings all the damn time and felt entirely too much pressure to stay late, work on the weekends, or God forbid you to try to multi-task in those meetings! I'm blessed in my current position that I don't have that problem - but I think a person can be much more intentional about time is scheduled during the work day.

In the first place, you know the saying, "if you don't control your calendar, it will control you." So control it. You need work time? Schedule it. Call it just that: WORK TIME. I currently hold blocks of time as work-time, and in the "location" section of Outlook, I write down what I want to get done during that section of time. Work on the science grant, clean up email box (more on that later), Web Site Changes, clean desk, etc. And I try to do this at least one full week in advance so that I don't get overwrought with meetings before I save time for me. Don't fill your entire calendar lest you get in trouble for not being available. I look at my recurring meetings first - which days are my busiest meeting days and which days are very open. I usually schedule a 2-3 hour block at a time, at least 2-3 times each week. My current supervisor actually really likes this strategy and has begun to try it for herself.

If you are working for a company who schedules a great many meetings, you may need to speak with your supervisor regarding your need to schedule more work time. Especially if those recurring meetings are frequent. Give yourself a month to get used to the meeting schedule, and then you can approach your supervisor about options you have to delegate or remove some of those meetings from your calendar.

Additional Priorities and Opportunities
"Instead of saying, 'I don't have time,' try saying 'it's not a priority' and see how that feels."
--Courtney Carver

Working in higher education, I haven't always had the luxury of getting to decide for myself what's important. But in considering how you are spending your time, think about the extra things you take on in addition to your regular work. I'm going to be the first person who tells you that getting involved outside of your job is super important - for the professional development, making friends, networking, etc. But you may have to limit that involvement or consider that it's part of your free time instead of your work time. And make choices that sustain this.

I was very active in my professional association once I moved to California, and I carried that with me a great deal. I chose to have much of my social life connected through that organization...and I chose to be involved rather than going to a movie or doing other social things on the weekends. When I became a runner, I had to alter further some of these choices of how to spend my time outside of work - I saw fewer movies and was less involved in my professional association. And then, during times when my volunteer work was really busy, I just was not training for races.

But sometimes you really do need to choose between the extra work/responsibility and your home life. Saying "no" means that you can say "yes" more often. The quote above is indicative of knowing what projects mean the most to you. Which extra responsibility will you enjoy the most? Which project will aid in the advancement of your career, or help you to work with someone new and influential? Really consider this before taking on a new project or committee. It's better to do a couple of things really well than have mediocre performance in a ton of things.

Of course...there's always the "other duties as assigned" clause in many of our job descriptions. You know what I'm talking about, they're usually at the very bottom of the page, that "catch all" which seemingly gives your supervisor or other managers the option to throw extra projects at you...this can be tricky to navigate, especially during times when you are short staffed and surviving budget cuts. Be honest with your supervisor if you feel overwhelmed, and remember that you must communicate with peers and committee members who are sharing the workload with you.

It should also go without saying that you ask permission to take on professional association committee work before you volunteer. It's a common courtesy, and it gives your supervisor the chance to assist you with skill sets and connections that could assist in your new project or committee work. If they've been in your field for some time, they could even have great suggestions and recommendations for you, some that you hadn't considered.

Take advantage of flexibility or find room to be flexible within the job day
If you have the luxury of a flexible work day, then you can make room for longer breaks or be creative with your lunch hour or come in later/leave earlier when you need to. Do you have the ability to work from home now and then? Will your supervisor allow that? If you are lucky enough to have one of those gigs, make sure you keep it in perspective and get your shit done. Don't take advantage or take for granted, because you might lose it!

The flip side of this is having no flexibility – zero, zilch, none. Your work day is rigid, and you have meetings, meetings, meetings. That's tough. You may need to build in buffers between your meetings. Don't schedule back to back meetings. Start a meeting at 9 am, it's over at 10:30, don't schedule another meeting until 11 am. And then don't go back to the office and work before the next meeting. Take a walk, get a cup of coffee, and breathe. Control your calendar, or it will control you.

How to put your work day into perspective
You know what? It's just work. It's meaningful for you - you put your heart and soul into it. But it's just work. If you can't draw the line between where your job ends, and you begin....that might be a problem. The big thing for me was being able to realize that I was no longer going home angry. That was a beautiful thing. I took my work home - in an emotional manner - for such a long time. I would be so frustrated with the tough day and/or negative students and/or a rotten staff meeting...I'd internalized so much of it, and it made me angry. So I needed to draw that line and say, "I'm going home, and I'm going to be me." That's it.

You may need a buffer from your work day into your home life. If you are a live-in professional, this can be difficult. I'm lucky to have figured this out for me in my current vocation. For two years I was a walking commuter and listened to podcasts on my walk to and from work. Currently, I commute by car but the travel time is about the same. I still listen to podcasts but have been on a mad audiobook phase for the past three months. Jen Sincero just rocks. This usually clears my mind from any daily funk and puts me in a lighter mood when I get home. Some of you may have very long commutes and so time in traffic further complicates your transition time. Loud music may turn into road rage, so I recommend podcasts (again - I'm a big fan), audiobooks, comfortable/slow music. Even something that you are familiar with and can sing along. But any drive home can feature these things, and you really only need a few minutes to make it happen.

During that transition time (otherwise known as your commute home), let go of everything that happened at work that day. The work day is over. What are you looking forward to once you get there? Spouse or significant other? Family, kids? Dogs? Someone making an amazing dinner for you? A very nice glass of wine and a fire? Focus on one of those things to think about while you let your work day go...and SMILE. Even if you have to force yourself to smile. Because even just smiling will brighten your mood.

Learning how to "unplug" and separate

Even as I'm writing this, I know good and well that I struggle with this myself. My husband and I have smartphones and tablets, and I often bring my work laptop home. So I myself am not the model of unplugging. Writing for *The Bulletin*, Sarah Comstock addresses the fact that technology has been a double-edged sword. Advances are helpful and convenient but "have placed an enormous burden of relentless pressure on people as expectations rise in parallel with the speed of technological progress." Computers and gadgets are suddenly able to do just about anything; as human beings, we need to recognize that *we can't do everything*. Being able to get away from our devices and technology is paramount to finding work/life balance.

In the first place, the main reason we add our work email to our phones is for convenience and flexibility. Having that connection allows us to respond to certain requests maybe between meetings, or while otherwise occupied. It's most certainly not meant to keep us from our families or friends or to occupy our downtime. You pull out the laptop with the intention of doing some personal research, or maybe you are checking your bank account, and the next thing you know you're opening Outlook and responding to emails. Suddenly a 15-minute task turns into an hour, or two. Next, there's the itching desire to "quickly check email" while you are at a restaurant with your significant other or friends and there you go again - you get caught up in an email chain of crap that clearly could wait until the next day.

Does any of this sound like you? It's me, too, much of the time. Some different strategies to consider include:

a. Do a "detox" from some of the apps on your phone that suck up your time. These apps could include social media, games, fitness, or sports viewing. Based on a challenge I learned about on the Rich Roll podcast, for the entire month of June 2015, I took all social media off my phone. I did not check in anywhere; I did not tweet or post on Facebook, there were no new Instagram shots in my feed. That gave me some focus when spending time with family and friends - it was nice to just be with them and not otherwise occupied with distractions.

b. Consider whether your employer requires you to have a department-issued cell phone; and if your institutional culture dictates that you have access to your email all the time. One of my previous institutions did require a department-issued phone with work email intact. I received compensation for this, but it was expected that email notifications be turned on and the focus is on staying up to date with all communication.

Thankfully, that is not the current culture for me. I do have work email on my phone, but notifications are turned off; and, in fact, from time to time I think about removing work email from my phone because I'd just as soon not have to worry about it. But given that my boss has work email on *her* phone, I model that example. And our classified staff members are not required to have email on their phone.

If the culture of your institution or your department requires this - don't be a rogue employee for the sake of balance. But consider other ways that you can ensure that your work email doesn't dominate your device. Are you able to turn off the work-related phone on the weekends? At night? Talk to your supervisor about expected response times? No one can check email 24 hours a day and still expect to be bright-eyed and bushy-tailed at the office.

I'll cover this in another chapter as well, but try to keep your email at the office from dominating your day. I'm doing the best I can to open, read, and respond/delete to my emails as soon as I get into Outlook, and then close the application until the end of the day. I try to be at "Inbox Zero" before I go home. This ensures that I'm not wrongly multi-tasking during the work day (which, by the way, there is no such thing as multi-tasking) or spending too much unnecessary time on email when there are projects to complete.

A new strategy I'm employing is not to open my email until I return from my lunch break. This was something my current supervisor read about in an article, and I really love the reasoning behind it. When you start the day with email, you are letting others dictate your priorities rather than controlling these yourself. If the email truly is an emergency, that person will call you or come find you. Hit up your main priorities in the morning, and then settle into the questions after you get some food. I'm enjoying the productivity of my morning and the peace of mind I feel because I'm not letting others dictate my work day.

Essential to unplugging is the notion of separating. Don't multitask your work and your life. Unless part of your job is posting to social media daily, leave all that stuff at home during the work day. Do you need Facebook and Twitter open on your computer while you try to write that report (or get your email to "Inbox Zero")? In his book, Deep Work, Cal Newport suggests "the overuse of social media unwittingly cripples our ability to succeed in the world of knowledge work." Social media is lots of fun, but in the office, it's just a diversion that's keeping you from finishing your vital tasks. The sooner you get your stuff done, the sooner you get home.

If you must make a personal call, check in with your significant other, or connect with your family; you can do so by taking a quick break and making your call from the break room or outside.

Know Your "Talents" and "Strengths"

I'm a huge advocate of personality assessments - I find them to be fascinating and helpful. I was a Myers-Briggs junkie for years. I completely identified and owned my ENFJ status. But I could appreciate how some folks felt about Myers-Briggs putting them in a "box" and assigning a label.

When I moved to California, my supervisor introduced me to the world of StrengthsQuest. In 1998, Dr. Donald Clifton, Tom Rath and a team of scientists at The Gallup Organization created Strengths Psychology - an assessment styled to focus on strengths rather than weaknesses. Out of this became the online assessment tool known as StrengthsFinder 1.0; and an update hit in 2001 with the book Now, Discover Your Strengths. Gallup surveyed over 10 million people on the topic of employee engagement to come up with the 34 signature talents - and that's what you learn about yourself when you take the StrengthsFinder online assessment. Anyone can do this by purchasing a new version of Tom Rath's book Strengthsfinder 2.0. This book is available on Amazon and booksellers everywhere. You can get it brand new from between $10-$19 depending on the time of year.

This assessment was a total life changer for me. Suddenly, I was able to focus on the areas of my life that were successful, came naturally, and kept me engaged with my workplace. The book outlines many examples of both famous, high achievers and regular folks like you and me. Being a good shoemaker versus being a good salesperson of shoes. Having a great long game in golf using your driver rather than being an exceptional putter. Being skilled at developing software rather than hardware. The examples go on and on. In the book, Rath states, "You cannot be anything you want to be - but you can be a lot more of who you already are."

Having this wisdom in my life really changed things for me. Understanding my five talents and how they work for me in my place of business helped hone my abilities in Senior Management for the first time in my life. Embracing my ability to build a team of being a solid problem solver. Consistently developing my desire to take something good and make it great. Releasing the concept that I will never be a good data person. Once I really channeled the way I did my job into these talents helped keep me engaged at work - and _really_ emphasized why work-life balance was so important for me.

No matter where you are in your career, I highly recommend that you pick up this book and learn about your Signature Talents. Once you take the assessment, you can also pick up copies of the older Strengths books as well as the companion strengths books, which are all listed in the resources section at the end of this book.

Create your own Professional Development
I come from a culture where for years, decades, there had been a budget in every department for Professional Development. In higher education and student affairs, this usually meant having funds to attend a professional conference. And there was usually a delineation between the Regional Conference and the National Conference, but everyone could usually choose from at least one. I've worked at places where Senior Management had a particular affinity towards one particular professional association - so if that's the conference you wanted to attend, it was easy to get permission. Professional Development equaled Conferences, and that was about it.

When the market tanked in 2008, budgets had to be cut. And of course, conference travel/professional development funds had to be drastically reduced or altogether eliminated. At my place of employment, my team was frustrated and disappointed, but I found a way to make this more palatable for them.

If you are a manager with a team, you can do this exercise at the beginning of your calendar year/fiscal year, whenever it's the beginning of a new cycle for you. If you are in higher education, this is a great exercise to fold into your early semester training or retreat.

We would sit down as a team and talk about the following things:
a. Current issues or trends in our field
b. Specific skill sets that we want to learn and adapt
c. What are the next steps in our careers and how to plan for them?
d. Anything else they want to put on the table

We brainstorm, and everyone writes down their own answers to these various pointed questions. We put everything up on a white board or sheets of paper on the wall. And then we identify themes. We would identify at least 7-8 themes that would be developed into Professional Development Monthly Sessions. And from there, every team member volunteered to become the "expert" on that theme and provide a session for the team. Maybe they would ask another professional on campus to come talk to us; maybe they would identify a book we all should read and discuss, or maybe they would research the topic or trend and bring us new information.

Regardless of what they chose to do, each team member benefitted from:
a. Doing research
b. Networking
c. Presenting
d. Asking pointed questions in order to fully understand a topic or idea

And as far as I'm concerned, this annual Professional Development Curriculum did more for my teams than any regional or national conference.

If you don't manage your own team, or you don't have a supervisor who is willing to do this with you or your staff, then you have a little bit of work to do for yourself. And you can build your own personal curriculum on skill sets that you want to create for yourself.

Do a Google Search topics of interest
I enjoy trying to find articles or research or new books and media on things that interest me. I spent a great deal of time researching articles for this book, especially on the generational differences. You can find everything from Huffington Post articles to scholarly articles, and you might even find someone's doctoral dissertation.

Do a search on the Amazon Kindle Store for topics of interest
Or, just on Amazon or any bookstore for that matter…you might really be a traditional reader and need the copy itself. A friend of mine turned me on to Paperback Swap which is a great place to trade and buy used books. I've also recently started up with audiobooks again, and I love listening to them on my way to and from work every day.

Basically, what I'm trying to tell you is that you should just read more. Period.

Carve time each day for working on your curriculum
You might have a chance each day to schedule a 30-minute block of time to pursue your development plan at your place of business, but you also may need to make this a priority in your personal time. I have tried to read for 15 minutes every night before I go to bed. It also helps me unplug from my devices and settle in.

Join local organizations that align with your interests
There are many organized groups in your communities that may be useful and developmental in your professional development. Let's say you have an interest in public speaking or professional presentations…see if there's a Toastmasters group nearby. If you are interested in learning accounting, maybe there's a free course at the local community college or offered by a firm or CPA office.

Reflection Questions:
1. Which of these hacks/habits/DIY fixes seem the easiest for you to try right now? Which feels like the hardest?
2. Write down three books that you'd really like to read in the next month.
3. What will be your "buffer" that you select to separate your work day from your home life?

Chapter Four:
Relationships

The Significance of Support Networks
"Surround yourself with people who support you. Find champions."
--Sarah Gavron
"When you find what you love, and you find people that will support you, you're living the dream whatever you do."
--Cole Swindell

I love both of these quotations because they embody the spirit and good feeling when you know there's someone at the office who's got your back. Everybody needs a cheerleader in their life - both at work and after work.
The role of your support network includes:
Validate your decisions
Listen to your frustrations
Encourage your development
Help you see the other side

I highly recommend the book <u>Vital Friends</u> by Tom Rath. Rath has written a plethora of books on various aspects of personal development as it relates to our vocation. All his books get to the heart of work-related issues, especially in one of my very favorite books, <u>Strengthsfinder 2.0</u>, which I'll reference later in the book.

In <u>Vital Friends</u>, his research and writings discovered that "people who have a 'best friend at work' are seven times as likely to be engaged in their job." The opening page of his book includes nine crucial questions to ask when determining these people in your life. Once again, if you buy the book brand new, you will get a code for an assessment that can put these ideas into perspective from a scientific point of view.

I never consciously sought these people out before - as I go back and reflect on all of my different jobs, it's pretty easy to identify those individuals who served as my vital friends. Early in my career, when I was a live-in professional, the lines between having *best friends at work* and *outside of work* could be blurry at times; if your social network is also your work network, then you may be out of balance.

There's another word for this Vital Friend relationship: your "work spouse." If you google this phrase, you will find all sorts of interesting articles on the dynamic. Some are humorous, others quite serious. Some make connections to whether or not your work spouse or vital friend becomes your life partner. This can totally happen; and if it does, congratulations. But I think I already described my own personal bias about having a significant other in your field.

With all that being said - who is that person at your place of business who you cannot live without...and who, if they left your organization, would make you unsatisfied? Just some thoughts for reflection. Like I said, we all need a cheerleader in our lives.

Now let us get outside the place of business...and talk about that support network outside of the cubicle. One of my favorite films from the 90's is THE PLAYER, directed by Robert Altman and starring Tim Robbins as a film executive. There's a scene that really resonates with me in terms of having that separation from work and life. The scene unfolds as a group of Robbins' colleagues are at a Power Lunch, and everyone is talking about the movie business. Robbins seems flustered by this and says something to the effect of, "why do we always talk about the business when we go to lunch? We're educated people; we can talk about other things, right?" There's a fairly long, awkward pause before everyone cracks up laughing. No one had anything else to say! I do tend to chuckle during this scene; but in the grand scheme of things, it's really not funny.

How can you live a life of balance when you can't emotionally and mentally remove yourself from the workplace?

My first year after graduate school, in a live-in position as a Hall Director, this wound up being a very big deal for me. There was a core group of us who did a variety of activities together on a regular basis; we enjoyed each other's company at work and outside work. There had come a time late in the academic year when I disagreed with one member of that core group. I became frustrated with the work relationship, and it spilled over to the friend relationship. Just like that, my social circle became strained, and I spent less time with those colleagues outside of the work place. That experience made me feel very alone at times. I had just gotten married and was living very far from my friends from graduate school and my family. I had my husband to turn to, but I did need at least one more person in my life to lean on.

From that day forward, I realized I needed to seek those people out and develop those relationships. It wasn't always easy to do. There were instances where I was living and working in a city where I already had friends, and that made the outside-the-work social circle development much easier. However, I have worked in places where I never had that person outside the office. Most of the time, everything worked out okay for me. And in fact, one of my very best friends in the entire world is someone I met at work - but we found that we had enough things in common outside of our jobs, and it was very easy to talk only about those things when we would hang out.

Where do you meet people when you move to a new city and don't know a soul? There are dozens of places; you just need to be a little extroverted to find them.

*Find your preferred church, and meet people there.
*Find or create a "Meet Up" group over similar interests.
*Volunteer in an agency which aligns strongly with your values.
*Get involved with something like Team in Training - or any other organization that trains you to complete endurance events while fundraising for a cause. I met my current best friend through this platform and found a new hobby in the meantime.

A few years back, I read a book titled GLOW: HOW YOU CAN RADIATE ENERGY, INNOVATION, and SUCCESS, written by Lynda Gratton. I found an exercise in this book that I used for years in presentations for young professionals on how to expand your network. Using the following groups, try to name three people for each of these categories:

- Close friends who are similar to me
- Close friends who are different from me
- Acquaintances who are similar to me
- Acquaintances who are different from me

Then, for the 12 people you named, ask yourself these questions:
- Is this a relationship that fills me with joy?
- Is this a relationship in which I learn new things?
- Is this a relationship in I feel cooperative and trusting?

According to Gratton, "the key is to create value by achieving a balance between closeness and distance and between similarity and distance." Pretty cool stuff, if you ask me. But I truly believe that having these four different sets of people in our lives can help us further achieve balance in our networks. Try it yourself. Seriously. It can be really hard to find Career Bliss if you are blocked or distracted by things or people who aren't at your place of employment. These influences can greatly affect how you approach work (or recover from work). I want to outline just a few of these — the way you manage them can be the key to finding Career Bliss.

Personal/Romantic Relationships
"Never get so busy making a living that you forget to make a life."
--Dolly Parton

In my professional career, I've known many people who were, for all intents and purposes, Married to Their Job. The last thing they want to do is settle down with someone. The "work" is more important. In my earlier years, in particular, I met several women in mid-level management who fit this description. They had been single for years…they were also overweight and did not exercise…they took work home and aligned their identity with their day to day duties at the office. Even at that time, my late 20's, I thought of how unhealthy that was/could be. But I looked up to many of these women because I saw how close they were with their students - and usually, they were very popular on the conference circuit. They won awards, and they were constantly presenting interest sessions. Because…they were Married to Their Job.

I met my husband during my last year of graduate school. I was not even looking. He just sort of fell into my lap. Our courtship was short - he moved with me when I started my first post-graduate job, and we got married during my first year as a Hall Director. And the funny thing about our wedding…we actually got married so my husband wouldn't have to pay rent to live off campus. Our official, legal wedding took place at the conclusion of Hall Director Training; we got married on Labor Day, just before the arrival of the student staff. Even as I write this, I have to laugh about how even my (first) wedding was intricately connected to my place of employment. I have very fond memories of that event - and while we did later have a real wedding for our family and friends, we celebrate this anniversary over the March ceremony two years later.

Our first two years of marriage were tough because we were both learning how to be married and I was learning how to be a professional in my field. I made a lot of mistakes. I held on to choices and behaviors that were okay when I was a student...and there were times that my marriage suffered or my work suffered. Once my hubby and I figured out how to be married and put energy and passion into our work, we really became a better couple. But for a lot of people out there...it's tough to meet people outside of your job. And many of my former colleagues in higher education wind up dating each other because that's the social network and the people with whom you spend the majority of their time. On the one hand, I think that's the dumbest thing that a person can do - in my opinion, you should not ever get romantically involved with someone in your field, because in the end when you go home at night all you do is talk about work. On the other hand, having your life partner also be in your field can serve as an internal support network - the person you go home to every night fully understands what you go through and what you're feeling. For myself, I'm really glad that my husband is not in my field. I need the clear separation from my daily vocation, and I think I'm a more diverse thinker and problem solver with the partner that I have.

Troubles at work can affect your personal relationships and troubles at home can affect your job performance. Even with a counseling degree, I don't have a magic answer for how to solve this. In Chapter 3 I talked about unplugging and having a buffer between work and home. This is one way to mitigate bringing work stress back to your house. Another way is to put just as much energy into your play time as you do with your work time. Work Hard, Play Hard. And make a promise to yourself or your partner that you will not talk about work once you walk in the door.

What if you are struggling at home: problems with your partner, children, siblings, extended family, etc.? You may have a lot looming over you. It's important to keep those issues separate as well. When you leave your home, give yourself a mantra to prepare for the workday, and then be fully present in your job on those days. Put extra focus into your day to day duties and projects to keep your brain occupied. If you have a supervisor or manager that you trust, let her know that you are struggling and you may need some leeway with current projects. Lean on your Vital Friend(s), so they can support you.

Reflection Questions:
1. Do you have Vital Friends at your current job? Who are they? Why are they important to you?
2. Go ahead and do the exercise just referenced from the GLOW book.

Chapter 5:
How Many Ways Can You Be Away and Still Be Okay?

Vacation, Life Events, Sick Time. Or maybe you just have Paid Time Off. Either way, you'll be away from work every now and then. That's okay. It really is. Stop feeling guilty.

Vacation – All I Ever Wanted
"The ant is knowing and wise, but he doesn't know enough to take a vacation."
--Clarence Day

We American's don't get it. You've seen that Mastercard commercial with the kids on the bus saying "One More Day," and quoting stats about American's having something like over blah-blah-and-blah unused vacation days each year. I know people who are FORCED to take vacation late in the year because their accrued days don't roll over to the next year. What the hell is wrong with us?

"The Executive who brags about going years without a vacation is neither a valuable organizational member nor a role model."
--William B. Locander and David L. Luechauer

Look at Europe. Thomas Geoghegan of the New York Times (October 2, 2013) sites interesting facts about European vacation and productivity compared to the States. "Yes, thanks to the six-week vacations, the nights at the theater on Tuesday night, the idle Europeans turn out more per hour than we worker-bee Yanks." A. Pawlowski of CNN.com says, "Despite research documenting the health and productivity benefits of taking time off, a long vacation can be undesirable, scary, unrealistic or just plain impossible for many U.S. workers." (May 23, 2011)

Can this be traced back to the whole Horatio Adler thing? Work hard, and change your fate. You can be a self-made man. That's encouraging stuff, but Horatio Alder helped impoverished boys climb out of poverty - and many Americans who don't take vacation are too wrapped up in the notion that they have to climb the ladder, gain as much prestige in the office as possible, and be the best.

I agree with hard work, being a self-made person, and being the best you can be. But everyone needs to recharge their batteries. According to a 2013 study by the U.S. Travel Association, "most managers recognize the benefits taking time off from work provide to employees: higher productivity, stronger workplace morale, greater employee retention, and significant health benefits. But nearly 34 percent of employees surveyed indicated that their employer neither encouraged nor discouraged leave, and 17 percent of managers considered employees who take all of their leave to be less dedicated, according to the survey's findings." That's ridiculous.

There's certainly an unwritten rule in Student Affairs (and particularly in housing) that there are certain times of the year that you just don't request vacation time. For me, as a housing professional, that pretty much meant May and August. And eventually, May, July, and August. And eventually, May, July, August, and February. Or March. Depending on recruiting season and which placement conferences you had to go to. There was a part of my early career in housing where it was just implausible for me to take more than a long weekend off at a time. I can remember taking a full week off during Spring Break of 1998 and returning back to work exclaiming, "I will NEVER take a full week off again!" I was so crazed upon my return. Obviously, I got over that...I don't mince words over more often than not taking one long weekend every month...but I'll never feel guilty about going on vacation ever again. EVER.

Sick Time
Sick Time is yet another benefit offered by our employers, and there is a good reason why. Sometimes, we get sick! We don't feel well. We shouldn't be at work. It's okay. Stay home and get better. Is it really worth it for the entire office to now catch a bug because you felt too guilty to stay in bed or go to the doctor? That's just selfish. Don't go to work sick.

I'm also going to tell you about a little thing I learned during my college housing years that we called The Mental Health Day. I had Mental Health Day policies at two of my institutions – they were unwritten policies, but they did exist. And yet, I hesitate to tell you about them, because they are slightly unethical. Because you may have to lie.

Working in college housing could really be high stress at times, and you can't always squeeze a vacation day in there. So every now and then, I might call in sick and stay home. I wasn't sick; I was taking a Mental Health Day. In which I might sleep in, get a massage, binge-watch television while eating Fig Newtons, go to the beach, whatever was needed to find my center again. And go back to work the next day feeling invigorated.

Let me be clear that I'm not telling you to call in sick every time you feel tired or stressed out. The Mental Health Day should not be taken for granted or overused. Be smart, people.

Life Events
"People to whom nothing has ever happened cannot understand the unimportance of events."
--T.S. Eliot

At one of my previous employers, Life Events were what we put on the table when we wanted to get out of a certain weekend on-duty. And these were specifically defined, like weddings, graduations, family reunions, big deals that were planned in advance. These Life Events can be pre-scheduled, of course; but they can also fall right on your head and become a real problem or distraction. Life Events are basically any major event or situation that can change a person's status or circumstances. These can be positive or negative, and they usually do consist of a certain amount of stress.

The previously scheduled life events, as mentioned above, get put on your calendar far enough in advance that you can prepare for them. But you may very well need a staycation or a long nap after they conclude. And we haven't even considered if the life event is something you are attending only, or actually participating in. For example – are you attending your sister's wedding, or are you actually getting married? Are you going to see your nieces graduate from high school, or are you actually graduating with your doctorate? How you are connected to the Life Event will dictate the amount of downtime you'll need when it's over. Make sure that you have also prescheduled in that buffer between the Life Event and when you return to work, so you aren't a crazy person coming in at 8 am when you just got off the plane at 1 am, and you might still be a little tipsy from the wedding reception.

Life Events that take you by surprise because you weren't expecting them can be much harder to process. Death in the family, accidents, unanticipated health issues, a break-up or divorce, and so forth. Because you hadn't planned for these necessarily, the stress can be overwhelming and you may need to get some help. These are the times when those support networks, vital work friends, and relationships with supervisors need to step in and advocate. While a discussion with your supervisor to confirm how much time you need to rebound from your event may mitigate your stress, all those various Human Resources related details that you may or may not have paid attention to during orientation can be of use during times like these. Do you know how many bereavement days you have? Does your employer have a catastrophic leave bank, where employees can donate their sick or vacation time to help someone who needs to take additional unpaid leave? FMLA, The Family and Medical Leave Act of 1993, is a US labor law requiring covered employers to provide employees with job-protected and unpaid leave if necessary. Additionally, most employers these days have some form of Employee Assistance Program where you can find a counselor or support group to help you get through the situation and get your life back into alignment.

The most important thing to consider in situations like these is that you need to take care of yourself. Period.

Reflection Questions
1. Peruse your current employer's Human Resources website and get familiar with what kinds of leave are available to you if you need to use it.
2. Which positive life event would be most stressful for you to handle?
3. Which negative life event would be most stressful for you to handle? Who would you go to for support and guidance during this period?

Chapter Six:
Should I Stay or Should I Go?

At the beginning of this book, I told you that I hoped you would not need this chapter. Hopefully, you can just close the book now knowing that you're in a pretty good place in making Work "Work" for you, and you're on your way to that Career Bliss. But – if you need this chapter, let's see what I can do to help.

I've known many people during my career who have had to leave a position and find something else. Their health, wellness, mental needs, relationship, or other reasons called for this. Only YOU can make this choice...and if you don't, it could very well be made for you.

I've been counseled out of two jobs in my life. Both had their positive and negative sides, but I benefitted from both in good ways. The first time was when my university's department was going to take a big turn in a direction that was not necessarily aligned with my talents. My supervisor basically said to me, "you don't have to leave, but if you stay, you need to get better at this, this, and this." My strengths, talents, and joy instead stemmed from that, that, and that. So, I started job hunting. Mid-year, even. I didn't **have** to leave, but I was given a very conscious choice to choose my career trajectory, and I didn't want it to be where my current employer was going. I greatly respect my supervisor for giving me room to think about that choice and for being honest with me on where she wanted my department to be going.

The second time came from a basic miscalculation of the institutional and departmental culture...and the balance of this was sucking the life out of me. I had reached the point in my career where I did not want to work 60-80 hours a week, and my supervisor was very clear role modeling was the expectation. Not saying it, but definitely role modeling it. And eventually, he let me know that our current situation was probably not the best fit, for the department or for me. I had choices to make, as well as a soft landing, to fall upon. For this job search, I cast a very wide net in a small geographic area - which led me to leave the field of Student Affairs.

I reference the "soft landing" in my second example above. This was something I was very lucky to have. My supervisor arranged for me to have a yearlong position in another office on campus should I not get a job offer once my role in my current department had ended. One full year. That's a blessing. It was a blessing that I wound up not utilizing, thank goodness, but I consider myself very fortunate that my supervisor offered me a living for one year, even though it would not be with his department.

So I have just shared my two stories, both of which had mainly positive elements at play; unfortunately, you may not have those options. You may really have to leave, by your own choice, because your current position gives you no joy, sucks the life out of you, and makes you miserable.

I'm not going to lie - that's a huge risk. Leaving a seemingly stable job that makes you miserable is a huge decision and should not be taken lightly. Because unless you have a rich relative and a trust fund waiting for you, we all have to make a living. And this is more than just focusing on your craft before you squander it, etc. (referencing "The Cosmic Shame" from earlier in this book). The smart thing to do is find a new gig before leaving your current one. Doing a job search is time consuming and requires a great deal of focus and effort. If you have a partner or family involved, you will have to make some big choices. My job searches always seemed to take me to different states or cities altogether (remember, for years I was only in search of The Perfect Job), but you may not want to do that. I mentioned above that I cast a very wide net in my job search, applying for every job I was remotely qualified for, even if I didn't understand it.

Choosing to leave, though, gives you opportunities and options as well. You can figure out a way to reinvent yourself and go after a new vocation, maybe something that's always tickled your fancy, or you decide to pursue the job at the company you'd always wanted to work for. If you have read this far and you need to decide between staying and going, then re-read Chapter 2 and really focus on your reflection questions.

How and when do you decide to notify your employer of your intentions? This is a tough call. In most of my previous positions, it was either suggested that I consider transitioning (see example #1 above), or I realized that this was not the best fit for me or I was seeking advancement. I was ten years into my career before I realized that I was seeking advancement. In most cases, it was very comfortable for me to tell my current supervisor, "I'm going to look for a new position." But in two situations, I kept my search a secret. Once was because I was so miserable that I wanted to find something new and just get out. I don't recommend this, as it left me leaving a position and a department-high and dry. I had colleagues and vital work friends who I respected, and it was hard to put that extra work on them. I gave notice as soon as I was hired for my new job, but basically three weeks later I was gone. In the second case, I was informed by a work friend that announcing my intent to find new employment would destroy my current situation. This was apparently a culture where it was expected that you love working there - the thought of seeking a job elsewhere was "treason." Okay, that's a strong word. But that concept frightened me, and I looked for work secretly. By the time I had a job offer that excited me, my current supervisor had left our office - so the person I had given notice to was actually my colleague, and the announcement was easy. And my start date at the new job gave me plenty of time to help transition the department so that they could work with a small staff while hiring replacements.

Again, please keep in mind that my situations are merely examples and in so many cases I was very lucky and the stars aligned for me. To be fair to your current employer and team, it is the right thing to do to inform someone of your intent to job search. When you get an offer and accept, it is the right thing to do to give at least one month's notice. And to support your current department and not burn bridges, it is the right thing to do all you can to close out your employment and duties with integrity and balance.

Conclusion

Perfect happiness, great joy, oblivious to everything else. This is the definition of bliss. To have Career Bliss means you are going to work just loving that job and what you get to do every day. Many of us struggle to get there, but hopefully, there were stories and suggestions in this book to help you get closer to that state.

If you Google quotations for "Life is Too Short," you get a plethora of poignant, funny, and inspirational things. Quotations like,

"Life is too short to blend in." Paris Hilton

"Life is too short to be miserable." Rita Mae Brown

"Life is too short to do the things you don't love doing." Bruce Dickinson

I love all of these and hope that you do, too. I wish all of you the best of luck in finding your Career Bliss. No one can define it but you. No one can recognize it except you. And only you can ensure that it happens. So go for it. Life is too short.

www.ingramcontent.com/pod-product-compliance
Lightning Source LLC
Chambersburg PA
CBHW020712180526
45163CB00008B/3058